PETERLOO PREVIEW 3

Peterloo Preview 3

EDITED BY HARRY CHAMBERS

PETERLOO POETS

First published in 1993
by Peterloo Poets
2 Kelly Gardens, Calstock, Cornwall PL18 9SA, U.K.

Printed in Great Britain by
Latimer Trend & Company Ltd, Plymouth.

This anthology © Peterloo Poets 1993

Individual contributions © Colin Archer, David Pell Goodwin,
Diana Hendry, Frederick Jones, Joan McGavin, Graham Seal.

**A CIP catalogue record for this book is available from
the British Library**

ISBN 1–871471–42–7

Supported by

ACKNOWLEDGEMENTS:

COLIN ARCHER: 'Chanson', 'The Operation', and 'Party Time' were first published in *Other Poetry*. 'Cast-offs' and 'The Wedding Cake' were first published in *Outposts*. 'Playtime' was first published in *Literary Review*. 'Mumbles' won 1st prize in the Berkshire Word for Word Poetry Competition 1989 and was first published in *Writers on the Loose*. 'Time Lord' and 'Singer of the Descant' won joint 1st prize in the Aberystwyth Open Poetry Competition 1990 and were first published in *Poetry from Aberystwyth V*. 'Armorial Bearings: Autumn' won 1st prize in the Bournemouth International Festival Open Poetry Competition 1991 and was first published in *Festival Poetry 1991*.

DAVID PELL GOODWIN: one poem in the selection was published in *Orbis*.

DIANA HENDRY: 'Piano Lessons' and 'In Defence of Pianos' were first published in *Critical Quarterly*. 'Funeral Dance' was first published in *Encounter*. 'The Body's Vest' was first published in *The Spectator*. 'Soliloquy to a Belly' was first published in *Poetry Dimension Annual 5*. 'Our Grendel' was first published by *The Mandeville Press*. 'Mental Patients in Peace Time' was first published in *Prospice*. 'Soliliquy to a Belly' was included in the anthology *Purple & Green: Poems by 33 Women Poets* (Rivelin Grapheme). 'Funeral Dance' won the 1976 Stroud International Poetry Competition. 'The Homely Pigeon' was short-listed in the 1985 Arvon Poetry Competition and published in the 1985 Arvon Anthology. 'Making Connections' was runner-up in the 1990 Manchester Open Poetry Competition adjudicated by Carol Ann Duffy.

FREDERICK JONES: 'Congreve's Balsamic Elixir' and 'The Institution', together with three other poems not included in the present selection of Frederick Jones's poems appeared (as a winning entry in the 1991 Northern Poetry Competition) in the anthology *Northern Poetry Two* (Littlewood), and 'The Institution' also appeared in *Weyfarers*. 'Cairns' was awarded the Felicia Hemans Prize for Lyrical Poetry for 1992, and was published in *Poetry & Audience*. 'Loose Change' and 'Mandelbrot' were first published in *Scratch*. 'Hidden Pond' first appeared in *Poetry Nottingham*, and 'Getting on at Chingford Station' in *Staple*.

JOAN McGAVIN: 'Torn-Word' was published in *P.E.N. New Poetry 1*, edited by Robert Nye (Quartet Books, 1986). 'Expectation—Après Emily Dickinson' appeared in *Posterpoems*, edited by Professor Isobel Armstrong (University of London, 1990). 'On the Anniversary of the Death of George Herbert' appeared in *Footnote 2* (Winchester: The Schools' Poetry Association, 1984) and was published in *The Scotsman*, 1985. 'Lost Properties' was published in *The Scotsman*, 1985. 'Stuck in Highcrown Street' appeared in *Mandeville's Home Truths* edited by Peter Scupham and John Mole (The Mandeville Press, 1987).

GRAHAM SEAL: 'Man into Billiard Ball' and 'Pioneers' were first published in *Outposts*. 'Man into Billiard Ball' was subsequently included in the Borestone Mountain Poetry Awards anthology *Best Poems of 1976*. 'Pioneers' subsequently appeared in *How Strong the Roots* (1981) edited by Howard Sergeant. 'The Bloody Horse' was first published in *Transatlantic Review*. 'They Call it Education' was first published in *Tribune*.

Contents

Colin Archer, born in 1931, was brought up in London and North Wales. He has been, in turn, a Company Secretary, local government administrator, Social Work Director, mature student (with a top First in English), writer (in many genres), and Creative Writing Tutor. He recently completed six months as Writer-in-Residence at a Hospice. He started writing poetry in 1981, has won many competitions, and appeared in a number of magazines.

Colin writes: "Most of my material, so far at least, comes from my own family life and from work with people suffering stress and distress. Increasingly the poetry itself involves interaction between the personal and the professional, the 'I' of the poem embracing more than the merely personal. The poetry in this selection is centrally concerned with the passage of time, but this is a passage in which I find not only losses to be mourned and terrors to be recalled, but also human spirit, wit, and hope.

"For me, poetry is a 'learned difficult art', most notably in harnessing the power of words to be deeply suggestive if not downright ambiguous, and the power of form, especially in the positioning of line breaks. The difficulty of the art leads me into constant practice, false starts, and something akin to 'pain' barriers when an incipient poem refuses for day after day to be shaped. Finally, though, it is an art which I cannot now be without."

Colin Archer

Chanson

Off-season, the pier reaches out
Into the dawn mist, one night angler
Still sleeping in the doorway
Of the Oceanic Bar. In the mud below,
Two grave figures are digging up worms.
I grip the rail, cast thoughts to the wind
With little hope of response

The pier is stripped as if for something
Serious: candy-floss banished,
Palmist packed away with her booth,
Deckchairs secreted under tarpaulins
Until little distracts from the sheer
Engineering—magnificent, yet petering out
In a few abandoned stanchions.

There is a yearning here for completion,
And I gaze into the deceptive mist
As if expecting another pier to emerge—
Reaching out from the opposite shore,
Steadily extending until we connect—
True to within a few thou'—
Forming a proper bridge—

With you zig-zagging towards me
On your ramshackle bicycle, singing.

Time Lord

Surreptitiously,
To save us all from the sin of lateness,
He'd set every clock in the house five/ten minutes fast:

For years we stood drenched at the front of bus queues,
Arrived to empty playgrounds, dawdled to parties,
Until we gradually dared to make allowances,

Whereupon he started sliding all the minute hands
Still further in the direction of Doomsday,
And we resolved to trust nothing but the kitchen radio.

But soon—after the usual Saturday night
Wind-up—the radio batteries unaccountably died on us,
And every clock then started telling a different lie,

With father's pocket chronometer once again
Looming high above the whole household, clamped tight
With some kind of ultimate truth known only to him:

Until today, in my own time zone, waiting patiently
With the family, I glance at my digital quartz, guilty
That I did not order the cortege five/ten minutes early.

Cast-offs

My first visit for years
To my wife's nursery class:

A gap-toothed Princess greets me
In yards of our bridesmaids' tulle —
Twin girls peer from their tent
In teacher's old maternity smock —
A Martian now wears our daughter's mini
15" below the knee — while
I am stormed by a Commando
Flashing the wolf-cub medals
Won by our graduate son

And I find more even
Than the missing tie
Which my wife so hated
And which Miss must have
Confiscated for the Pirate

For this is her secret
Family History Museum
With its small-scale models
Of Mummies and Daddies
Recreating me and you

Here — in the tumult
Of serious play —
I think I recognise
Something discarded
With my own rompers

And can study the origins
Of future rag-men
And charity workers
Preparing to clear
Everything I possess
For a song

The Operation

Ten days of summer:
The sun does not draw me out.
Ten nights: I drink deeply
But am not refreshed.

Rooted in you so long
I have now been torn
From all sustenance:
How could I thrive?

The man in the green smock
Who separated us
Left traces of you
Clinging to every fibre.

As he delves and corrects
I—who must be sunk in you—
Am cast aside:
See how I wilt.

Party Turn

Traces of trifle
on her dead black habit
a pink paper hat
perilous on her cowl
Sister Dulcima
demonstrates the Tango
with the oldest inhabitant

    and her polished apple face splits with joy.

Sister Dulcima
stray grey hairs curling
in excitement
sits puffing beside me
and confides
in rich Spanish tones

    'There is a time for dancing and a time for prayer'

Compline is calling
but she pleads to the ceiling
for one more dance
eyeing with true faith
the somnambulant figures
backs to the walls.

Sister Dulcima
has been here since dawn
preparing the party
and did not have time
for morning prayers
so yet again tonight
will have to say

    'Forgive me Lord but I have been so very busy'

She plumps across
for Mr Benjamin, 91,
and no quick-stepper.

The Wedding Cake

'Their marriage had never been consumed'
— *Social Work report*

There had, of course, been that first peck at a cheek,
The nibbling of ears, the odd slightly salted finger,
All the pre-marital snacks that God allowed;
But afterwards there it was, massive between them,
Something they knew they could never get through
And soon could seldom even face —
Weighty, sickly-sweet, funereal with fruit
And with the gluttony of those shameful couples
Who gobbled theirs up in one week flat.

After dark they would whisper of ways around the thing,
Scheme to slip something more succulent to each other
Through the tiers, if only it was less forbidding;
Still, each Christmas, after a drink, attempted a sliver —
But under the royal icing, the rosebuds and the cherubs,
Mother's special mix just mouldered,
Slowly crumbled away, a hazard to health,
Until they gaze at each other across the starving gulf,
Two aged anorexics, eating their hearts out.

Armorial Bearings: Autumn

The civic pride of lions rampant
Gone to seed; roundels and chevrons
Threadbare where, last night, the salvia
Took a hint of frost; the crest
Of fleur-de-lys (feigned by alyssum)
Thinning fast; while that majestic scroll
(Lobelia set in silver sage)
Can manage only the limpest WELCOME now:
Heraldic summer's draining back to loam.

Around the square the traffic snarls
Past Boots, McDonalds, C & A; the car park
Flashes FULL as early Christmas shoppers
Worm their way to tills; plane trees,
Yellowing in the Precinct walkway,
Look more sickly than autumnal;
Sparrows gather, flutter, pause,
As if they too are plotting to migrate;
Computer spreadsheets catch a gust and fly.

Here on my lunchtime scribbling bench
('In Memory of Edith Hall JP')
I ripen with fruitfulness
Less disciplined than Tesco's shelves.
My heady mix of childhood Coxes,
Damson, Loxtons, Beauty of Bath—
Though misty now as Michaelmas—
Is ready to ferment to verse.

But these were never gleaned from loam
Or orchard: most were scrumped
From back-street markets, harvest hymns,
And Keats. So now I seek my bearings
Here, in a fading coat-of-arms:
No pageantry to blazon blood,
No poesing to saccharine decay,
Not autumn words but autumn in the flesh—
For here's Diana, clutching her yoghourt,
Spring in her step.

17

Singer of the Descant

'His name I know and what his trumpet saith'
Francis Thompson

The keen eyes of the late treble saw
So much: cracks in the face of the angels,
Holes worn in lace and stone embroideries,
Those unshaven patches
In the puckers of his moist mouth
As he expounded the resurrection,
Announced a rousing recessional,
Then detained one or two for private tuition:
See, the dark mysteries of the word made flesh
In the hands of the priest.

Treated to his word-hoard, I for one
Could not always distinguish thing from act —
Doxology, censer, rubric, genuflexion —
Shoes gently aspiring
In the stale depths of his cassock
As he voiced deep concern for my faint faith.
Did I not feel certain stirrings? And yes,
I did sense something potent, mystic perhaps,
Beneath all those gilt artefacts
And his unstarched canonicals.

Had he noticed me flush as we sang that Lo
He abhors not the Virgin's womb,
And later, in libraries, secretly looking up
Abhor, and other disturbing recurrences —
Circumcision,
The *Odour of Sanctity, Extreme Unction,*
Proselytize, Postulant, even *Pedestal*
(The home he claimed for his holy *Pyx*),
Which I found somewhere
Between *Pedant* and *Pedestrian.*

I did not let him confirm me:
There was to be no laying on of hands
Beyond that one quivering half of a touch
In the ecclesiastical junk-room
From which I fled, voice broken,
Dumbly casting him as the Hound of Heaven
Turned on his Master,
This mild mongrel, held as tight as may be
By leash and collar, until today, in silence,
I thought I heard one calling, *Child*

Mumbles

Mumble is an embryonic conviction,
A preliminary draft, a disowning postscript,
A darkhouse stranded on a shipwreck of rocks;
Mumble is the missing link between Mumbo-Jumbo
And the Messiah, the unspeakable revenge
Of the growing child, the surly middle brother
Of Mutter and Murmur.

                             Mumbles congregate
Somewhere in the back row, survive on nasals,
Release sibilants, abandon vowels,
Implode words. Authority cannot abide
Mmbls, bans them from the media, yet mmbls
Still struggle not to be heard on next door's
Television

                   Ageing mmbls incline
To beards, set out on Sundays to impersonate
Priests, have half a mind to do something
And do it in their sleep; love smog, muffins,
Mushy peas; hate primary colours, sharp edges,
Most poetry, all Maths; cannot tolerate
Dumb insolence.

                   Mmbls are not to be
Pounced on: Mmbls are much misunderstood:
For beneath the moody mmbl and the begrudging,
The festering mmbl and the fearful, the depressed
And the indecisive and the apologetic, Mmbls
Are only human. A Mmbl cherished
May yet prove an angel unawares.

Playtime

Nagged to bring them together
Before they are 'put in their box'
We arrange our Grannies neatly
Side by side, adjusting awkward joints
Into semblances of comfort.

Two tiny bodies, bone-china heads
Crazed by wear, lolling back
Until the eyelids swivel shut; pursed lips
With no real words for each other
Save those we put into their mouths.

In the silence, the chatter of teacups
Lets slip their conspiracy —
For they have lured us here
To re-enact some outgrown scene
Under proper dolly tea-party rules

And to burden us with our childhood
Into the darkening night —
For when I take my one home to bed
She comes to dreadful life —
Triumphant that she has made me play her game

and that Ada (poor thing) (by the look of things)
Is set to be packed away first.

Teething

Nurse hands me your teeth 'for safe keeping'.
        They grin at me like death,
        Mimic the set of your jaw,
Defy me with your determination to survive

Anything. Nurse urges me to take them home
        To de-scale — as useful as Gran
        Boiling the water Doctor ordered
While he quietly checked that Grandpa had truly

Gone. Now life hangs onto that 'safe keeping'
        Until I recall Gran's teeth
        Grossly inserted by Undertakers:
Ave Maria playing over the shrunken mouth

Of a gorilla. This is an intimacy we've needed
        Not to share. One overnight
        To remove such stubborn stains
Will never do. Teeth lie in a cracked bowl and

Everywhere, chattering. I dream of donating them
        To the Third World
        To masticate hunger
While you wander, gummy, incomprehensible, tamed.

Nandini

This is you, Nandini,
Partying at fifteen months,
Beguiling all those honorary aunts
With your sudden eloquence,
Fit to bust with meanings
We can't quite capture.

We recognise something
Akin to words; incipient syntax;
The rising pitch of questions;
But this new language—
Full of vowels, diphthongs,
Sibilants, plosives —

> Is not (say half) English
> Nor (say the other) Bengali,
> Though we all (equally)
> Pretend to get your drift.

But you demand exact understanding,
And waddle away in disgust
To talk to someone your own size —
The kitchen pedal bin —
Who just stands there, open mouthed,
Taking everything in,

Until, unburdened,
You return to the hubbub,
Tip my old alphabet bricks
All over our feet,
And set about rebuilding St Pauls
Or rewriting Rabindranath Tagore
                    Or something.

David Pell Goodwin is a Zimbabwean born in Bulawayo, 1958. He served 18 months military service during Zimbabwe's bush war, then worked a passage to Rotterdam, cleaning and washing up. For six months he hitch-hiked around England and Europe. In 1982 he graduated from Cape Town with a B.Sc. in Surveying and married in 1983. He now has three daughters of 7, 5, and 2. Whilst in private practice as a cadastral (property) surveyor he studied English and Philosophy, gaining a B.A. by correspondence. In 1986 he joined the University of Zimbabwe as a lecturer. A Commonwealth Scholarship in 1988/89 enabled him to study for an M.Sc. in the U.K. He is currently Head of the Department of Surveying at the University of Zimbabwe where his special academic interests are land tenure and astronomy. A few of his poems have appeared in *Acumen*, *Orbis* and *Wasifiri*, though all but one of the present selection are appearing in print for the first time.

David writes: "My poetry has more than once been described as 'metaphysical'. I suppose that this is the scientist/engineer side of me that has always coexisted (somewhat disturbingly) with the artistic side, and which delights in the interconnectedness of words and ideas just as much as physical objects.

"Poetry defies precise definition, but I believe that at least two strands may be identified. The first is the central poetic idea (or ideas) of a poem which even without embellishment can move one extraordinarily. And the second strand is the language in which the germ of the poem is couched, the comparisons, images, symbolism, metre, rhyme, and so on. Both strands are essential, and of course there is no single formula for the balance between them, but the metaphysical poets perhaps placed more emphasis on the intellectual curiosity of the central poetic ideas than the form which contained them, while for some more descriptive poets the reverse may be true.

"Ultimately I see the function of poetry, or indeed any art, as being a springboard to take one from one quantum level of existence to another (or, if you prefer, to cause one to perceive life differently). This is hardly achieved by precise legal language, but the more evocative language of poetry calls upon a hinterland of ideas and associations already within the reader, and is simultaneously a catalyst and a springboard to combine and propel the awareness to different quantum states.

"Right through my life, wherever there has been a conflict between poetry and science, I have tried to let poetry prevail, because ultimately, of course, it is the more important of the two."

David Pell Goodwin

Large Shapes

Right now I would like to see massed leaves on trees,
Casting ink-pool shadows, like a child's finger painting.
I am tired of the winter filigrees.

I wish for cumulus cloud piles,
Blue with rain, like foothills. I have wearied
Of mist's wisps, and vaulted vapour trails.

I cast back for the elephant herds,
Which passed stamping and uprooting trees,
I have had my fill of squirrels and garden birds.

But branches, mist and birds are symptoms, I suppose,
Of a surfeit of small thoughts. My longing
Is for a global wisdom, a universal purpose.

Sermon from the Third World

I still look to the west at evening,
Though laser-etched silhouettes, like on imported notepaper,
Point to a sun which is setting.

Then my eyes blur, and focus sharply close by me
Where Africa is offering essences. I stare
At the stripped framework of a faith, centred on a thorn-tree.

The weedless, scuffed earth vouches for frequent use
In a way which weedless pews may not. This church is alive,
And around me even now life in the thatching-grass is diverse;

I have to move from one leg to the other
To stop mosquitoes settling. I know a heron-deliberate peace.
I am compelled by a unity with created order,

And contrast a Western church's Easter vigil
When I fought a wish to leave, to pray with natural things
Such as Christ in Gethsemane would hear and smell.

Paths converge here, which only the needy walk or ride,
And are brought to a focus at the acacia tree. A rusty sign
'World Gospel Church' is nailed with great nails to its side.

Rough words i rite

i wish i could be sure
That what i rite will teach a western mind
A truth he left behind
A thousand years before
i tried to rite the same as him,
i rote a poem on daffodils
But did not win a prize.
It is hard to think
Under this blazing sun.
They come out to this sun sometimes
To get experience, and tans,
And learn on us
Who are not in a position to say no,
And say we're lucky with the weather.
But i say its hard to think
Under this sun
And the goat's bells
And cicadas
Make me sleepy
And the bilharzia does not help.
Perhaps if i rote about goat's bells
And not daffodils ...
But surely the Western world
Has gone on past the point
Of goats and sleepy afternoons?
Our pleasures here are crude,
Rough words i rite.
Around me are thorns
No one has had time to clear,
Nor will for centuries.
Not measured in acres,
This thorn scrub goes for a hundred miles,
And the goats who eat it.
A rude pragmatism —
Don't clear the thorns, keep goats.
A sand path winds through the thorns,
It winds around trees
Because out here nature is as strong

As a mopane[1] trunk,
And man bends the path
Rather than chops the tree,
He gives way to nature still
Because he doesn't mind the extra time.
Maybe in Europe
Even if it's cool enough to think
And spell rite
They would cut the tree
Because of no time to walk round it
Or get off their bicycles.
And now it is the time
When the sun goes down,
And antelope and elephant are seen.
i wonder if in England
There are beasts and birds
If not as large who are as free:
How often can men say —
That beast does not need me,
Or even want my presence here,
And if i go it will carry on
And eat or walk or turn
As only it decides?
i think not often now.
i know as i sit here,
That these beasts need me not
And are not tame,
And i have to run when elephant or lion warn me.
i am thrilled
Because the sun is gone, and I feel
Thrilled
It is so cool
and frogs croak
And i have fresh hope
That the goat's bells may have meaning after all.
Even the bell is an intruder
On this natural scene.
It rings before the coming of those
Who can cut the stout mopane heart,
Who read it as a challenge

That it blocks their way,
Those who do not ride bicycles
And for whom shoe leather separates forever
Their feet from the earth.
But maybe they come out not only for the sun,
And deep down want to see a Jumbo or a Saddlebill
Who needs them like a hole in the head,
And because we are savages
And it doesn't matter if sometimes
They don't wear shoes.
Do they retrogress, who come?
Or can it be that they recall some ancient wisdom,
Mistakenly forgotten for a thousand years?

[1] *mopane:* an indigenous Zimbabwean tree with a dark, very hard centre.

Autumn Tree

Is it really unacceptable
To stare out of my office window,
To the yellow acrocapus[1], with its bulbul[2] and crow
And, the only ascending leaf, a golden oriole[2]?

I am not idle, my mind is housekeeping:
Repacking memories in new shelves
Labelled 'Autumn sights and smells',
And snipping and tying loose threads, and filing.

It's just that there is no visible activity,
And, except when a foot is shaken, or brow contorts
With each quick flurry of descending thoughts,
I am outwardly dead wood, an autumn tree.

[1] *acrocapus*: The Kenya coffee shade tree.

[2] *bulbul, golden oriole*: Southern African birds.

Avoiding the Fate of Rome

Of the opulence of that long weekend
On a white colonial farm, one of the cameos
Which remains with me now, is an evening
When most of the crowd drank beer and watched videos,

Or played 'Trivial Pursuit', while I
To their amusement, fixed a position
On the lush green *kikuyu*[1] lawn, using stars,
A wrist watch, and by theodolite observation.

In other words I calculated where on the globe
These trite activities were taking place,
With stars and constellations that Columbus used,
That ancient Egyptians knew: Betelgeuse,

Aldebarran, Vega and Canopus,
The Hyades, Pleiades, Orion,
Eridanus, Andromeda and Sirius.
Having done this to my satisfaction,

And while still pursued by a great distaste for ephemeral things,
I sat and played a guitar on one of the dew-damp deck chairs,
And harnessed music's ageless energy,
In the harmonics of the celestial spheres.

[1] *Kikuyu*: a variety of African grass.

Tenth Floor in Maputo (Mozambique)

They must know the phases of the sun like astronomers
These high flat dwellers,
Their lives revolving about washing,
Watching the seasons change,
Knowing that next month will bring a four o'clock shadow,
And damp napkins,
The month after sea-breezes
To dislodge flaking paint and pigeon feathers.
They must watch their city wind down about them,
To entropy's slow march,
Implacable as the sun.
Do they mark the equinoxes with cheap Portuguese wine,
These Galileos of today?
And muse over rubbish falling from their leaning towers?

The Mistral

They step off their bus,
Slightly tiddley, affectionate,
Vocal, not noticing us

Who for scores of generations
Have invested in land in this valley,
In permanent structures, plantations,

In labour and in children.
We have grafted and sown gifts
For our great grandchildren.

These people scorn primary production,
With its muck heaps and early hours.
They step back as only the very young

Onto growing plants.
Each gust of wind is a surprise
They clutch at their hats

Not seeing its pattern, and order,
Unaware of its predictable seasons.
It takes time, far longer

Than to click off a film,
To recognise an invisible current of air,
To expect it, give it a name.

Security of Tenure

I surprised landless labourers on a farm track,
So that they had to move quickly aside
To let my motorcycle pass.
Blinking, beside mounds of rich earth
With which they surfaced the road,
They were like emerging moles.
The earth, uncompacted, was
Heady as vacuum-packed coffee

With scents stronger than my exhaust stink.
It breathed a spirit of another place:
A mole tunnel, perhaps, with
The clipped, rank stumps of roots.
I caught the stirring breath of a brief moment,
Though it would leach out in time
Leaving impoverished aggregate;
More dust of Africa to rise from beneath wheels.

At lunch you men will sit under trees
In the diffuse, moving shadow of development plans.
And yet you have use-rights to certain things
Which I only come on accidently now and then;
Pre-dawn scents, of humus and drenched hay,
Sights of growing soya and potato,
And masasa[1] woodland, harbouring sounds
Of barbet[2] calls, and distant slow tractors.
Of all these things you have usufruct
For the duration of your stay on earth.
Your boundaries are like theirs;
Impermanent, undescribed by legend,
Contingent on the wind's whim,
Yet always richer within these bounds.

1 *masasa:* an indigenous Zimbabwean tree, renowned for its attractive red leaves in a certain season.

2 *barbet* (in this case the Black Collared Barbet): a species of Southern African bird. Male and female call together in a distinctive duet.

Physical and Spiritual

(On watching the Powerline Company's men on the light towers of Fontainbleau Township near Harare.)

1.
If there exist discretely
A grounded body and a mind with wings,
Then we must disallow a link
Between these radically opposed things.

2.
My survey gang
This Monday say nothing at all,
But only move more slowly
And do no action they are not ordered to do.
On high the powerline's men twitter
And like black-headed orioles in their yellow overalls
Whistle, and leap from bough to bough.
They are physically exalted by tens of metres,
And spiritually exalted too, we must surmise
Who watch them climb each distance twice for fun,
Do unergonomic pullups, and swing and shout.
My men advance, claim another metre of mud,
And hammer in another, blunt boundary peg.

To Philippa Pell

It must be like waking up on a Saturday,
Your first few weeks,
Hearing noises like someone striking a match
And making tea,
Or feeding horses next door with a clanking pail
Yet none of the sounds being imbued with the urgency
Of weekdays.

The cockroach on the cupboard,
And the fly on the cup's rim,
Are no more than moving points
For your new eyes to follow,
Unjudgementally.

Then, sleeping in my arms
As I scheme and plan,
You are as unconcerned
As the lilies of the field,
About today's raiment,
And tomorrow's meal.

Diana Hendry is a writer and journalist who lives in Bristol. As well as poetry she writes short stories and also novels for children. She was the 1991 Whitbread Children's Novel Award winner. In 1976 she won the Stroud International Poetry Competition. Her poems have appeared widely in magazines and a first full volume, *Skylark Research*, will be published by Peterloo Poets in 1995.

Diana writes: "Writing a poem is rather like having a conversation. Who with? Well, An Other. Sometimes a monosyllabic and reluctant Other, or a garrulously urgent Other or an angry Other. I think I am writing a poem. The poem thinks it is writing me. Over the years, I've come to think the latter is true. I know how I want the poem to go, the poem itself has other ideas. I think my better poems are the ones in which I allow the poem its own life.

"Thinking about the process of writing, the phrase 'letting in the light' came into my mind and I imagined a dark room and a woman drawing the curtains and saying 'Let's have a little light in here.' This seems to describe it. I don't start with anything as definite as darkness—perhaps with one line in the murk. And by 'light' I don't mean any grand illumination, but simply something that comes clear of the murk and which, for me, rings authentic.

"I became interested in poetry in my twenties when I was living near Liverpool and bought a book by Roger McGough. I leapt from McGough's poems to Horace's odes within a fortnight. The excitement I felt then, at finding this world of poetry, has never left me.

"I have written a number of books for children and some adult short stories. I like writing anything—even a shopping list—but nothing in life gives me quite the same charge as writing a poem."

Diana Hendry

The Body's Vest

Often I wish a thief would steal it,
or a tutting mechanic thumbs-down it,
or the police clamp it, or the Lord,
lowering a crane from the sky, up-reel it.

Each morning it waits to claim me,
demands oil and water, somewhere to go
and a hand to steer it. I confess I fear its
love of journeys; its Homeric glows shame me.

Others go by who put their lives on
every morning and sit inside them
and seem at home and know the way —
perhaps I've the wrong shape and size on?

Often I think I'd like to leave it,
an abandoned creature on the verge,
and 'casting the body's vest aside',
slip off on a slip-road and never retrieve it.

Our Grendel

There must have been something else but sea.
I try to remember the school, the church, the people

but the sea was the real professional — the rest
an amateur production. However vast the cast

the sea went one better, put on an epic,
a clincher. No need to go and check its

credentials. Trading under a host of disguises
the parent company was easily recognised.

The council built a groyne, a wall, iron-railed
and then, in autumn, all else failing

sent for the sandbags. We lived, I suppose,
as the Geats with Grendel, our sandy homes

full of Chinese chests and shrunken skulls,
restless with women and empty of sons.

Grandfathers outside the pub with salt white hair
sat on in uniform and stared out there.

Mental Patients in Peace Time

No war can excuse them,
the plebian mad
with their clichéd Christ dreams,
tended hems and marriages
immitatively bad.

Stunned by some lock on the brain
that sometimes twists,
they stare at mince and mash
on plates too thick
for cutting wrists;

or follow the trolley
that trafficks the wards,
that flies a brave nurse,
that plies clip-board cures,
that rattles a curse.

Manics blow in
in galleons of generous smiles —
here's to the electric cat
here's to Greek chorus girls!

They say this is a villa
in Wild Country Lane —
tell us its name.
Sacrifice,
damnation,
spendthrift waste
would give us status:
we are the unseasonably mad —
only relate us.

Piano Lessons

The terraced rows closed in and crushed you
in their jaws. At number ten, Miss Mildred
in her best front parlour, taught piano
on a neutered upright. All round
the walls were photographs of pupils who
had made the grade—past heroes of the
pianoforte, all capped and gowned and gone.
I found more promise in the piano's gold
and tabooed feet than in those haloed heads.

Somehow Miss Mildred smuggled in Beethoven,
fierce as sailor's rum. Quite drunk
on that illicit stuff, I'd pay my half-
a-crown and sidle from her spinster's den
prepared to find the neighbours risen
in outrage from their mothy beds.

In Defence of Pianos

(for Ben Kernighan)

In every alien place you find a piano —
schools, hospitals, prisons, asylums,
the homes of friends, your own front room.
Either they have been there forever
with a squeaky pedal and a dud B flat
or they breach-birth a window
and can't get back.

They should be extinct these standard uprights
lost in an iron-mongery moonlight
of genteel dust. The grand ones, got up
like mermaids in ebony velvet, bare
the awful symmetry of their jaws
in crocodile smiles
across the Albert Hall.

My Grös and Kallman, Berlin hausfrau, importantly
panelled and touched-up with brass, has two
timing pendulums engraved on her heart.
Her dreaming feet never touch the floor
and despite her homely Song-Book looks
she'll still flannel her hammers
with Wolfgang or Joseph.

O my frog-prince of furniture, I write
in your defence, having heard it said
that the lion's roar matches the desert,
the elephant's blare breaches the dark,
the bear can snarl at winter and snow
but man has only
a rented piano —

It is not widely known how far through the dark
of a night a piano can go, nor how
it can take to the streets in summer flight
so that hearing it ragging the silence you'd think
that man rented a forest to make a piano,
its falling pine needles
notes from home.

Soliloquy to a Belly

I have grown a belly.
It has swallowed up
my legs and arms,
even my head.

The government owns it.
Their man
comes to examine it
regularly,
like the meter.
I say 'I am behind it,'
but he has his union,
he has his schedule.

The old mothers
have come to my bedroom
to keep their vigil.
They sit and knit
straitjackets for daughters.
It's the species that matter,
it's all quite natural;
little husk,
you're for corn.

Along the street
the no-bellies walk.
In the space between
their breasts and legs
they've a squeeze
of desire, like picnic salt
in a twist of paper.
They'd like a belly
to sleep behind.

I'm afraid
my arms and legs
won't grow again.
It happens every day of the week,
you're not unique,
not even special.

I'll hem my sheets,
I'll let them read the meter twice,
I'll be nice to the midwife,
push when I'm told.
I'm lying in
behind this belly,
thin and cold.

Making Connections

Passengers talk through a porthole
to a man in a glass tank.
He has red-rimmed eyes
and a rubber stamp.

A scant metal bridge, humped
like the one on the Willow Pattern plate, spans
two platforms and a view
of the lost igloo city of cars
painted by children.

There's a photograph booth
(against loss of identity en route),
a news stand with 'The Plain Truth'
available free, in a dark corner,
and a row of telephone cotes
to home in the lonely.

I eavesdrop the news —
'He should be here at twelve minutes past four'
(Twelve minutes past, repeated,
as if repetition will bring him for sure) —
and wait for her

who is too young to be running over bridges
after love and trains —
this little go-between, this bridge-hopper
moonlighting between mother and father.

Small as the Chinaman on the plate
she waddles across the bridge with her case.
'Why didn't you telephone me yesterday?' I scold
waving love's big stick.

Funeral Dance

The spire is as perfectly centred
as the black and white priest in the doorway's arch.
Left of centre stands a large yew.
Six staunch bearers pace the path.
On the raw oak box, the shields of flowers
are heraldic crests that mock
our claims. Outside the gates
the mourners make two half moons.

Bach could have set it as a four-part fugue
but for the shapeless figures
in sullen grey who stumble, unsynchronised
after the coffin, breaking the dance,
draining the colour out of the grass,
making the priest seem sawdust and silk,
neutralising spire, yew tree, arch.

The Homely Pigeon

'Is it a pigeon?' I kept asking
the way one asks
is this the man I married
and what has possessed him
rushing in through the French windows
in grey gothic cloak
like a Shakespeare messenger?

Not the dove, swooping into the ark
of the moneyed apartment,
nor the quick light fligh
of Bede's bird through the hall.
This bird's fat and urban
and full of interrogating silence.

Is he the one?
The shy boy at the party
fingering his tie
now grown bold and daring
a cold gloat in his eye

disturbing.
Why did I not see
the artificial colouring of his breast
and beneath his shirt-tail
the appalling nail-lacquer pink
of his wrinkled legs
and loose-skinned claws?

I hold out bread
which he ignores.
He has no tidings
only a tag
ringed round his claw
in broken English,
the identity bangle
that tells his faith:

I am homely
I am homely
I am homely.

Skylark Research

I am the skylark researcher.
I am keening my ears for them,
eyeing people in the street,
asking 'Do you believe in skylarks?'

Nobody has seen one.
They look at me as if I've spoken
an exiled word.
I worry that skylarks have been expelled,
become dissident birds.

I try to pretend they are simply out
of fashion, like Shelley,
but secretly I am afraid
they have been hushed up,
or that something has happened to our hearing,
or that the hinge has broken on heaven's gate
and there's nothing to sing at,
or that they've worn themselves to a frazzle
singing their hearts out
at the blank sky.

Perhaps there's a change in our climate.
Perhaps the fluttering of cash cards
keeps them silent.
Perhaps they can't be heard above the din
of Help lines ringing through the night.

Possibly it is not yet dark enough
to set them off
and they are up there, arrowed
and waiting to wing from the bow.

Sometimes I imagine
a mass dawn vigil
and skylarks rising
up over the inner cities,
lifting the low skies
of England.

I romanticize.
I have nothing uplifting to say.
I am here to record
the comings and goings of the common lark.
I keep the word fresh for them.

I am the skylark researcher
Bulletins fly from my fingers.
I airmail the news.
It is my job to report
on what is beyond reach,
out of sight,
not spoken about,

there.

Frederick Jones was born in Middlesex and educated at the Universities of Newcastle, Leeds, and St. Andrews. He now lives in Liverpool, with wife and two children, where he lectures at the University in the Department of Classics and Ancient History. His prizewinning poems in the 1991 Northern Poetry Competition were published in the anthology *Northern Poetry Two*. Frederick Jones was the 1992 winner of the Felicia Hemans Prize for Lyrical Poetry. His first full volume, *Congreve's Balsamic Elixir*, will be published by Peterloo Poets in 1995.

He writes: "From earliest infancy we are exposed and respond to stimuli some of which (e.g. mothers) respond in turn, generating a sort of compound interest. Interaction is basic to the human state, transcending both the expression of feelings and communication. Put two people in a room and they will interact in all sorts of ways (observe the growth of human society, the development of the city, music, the concert-hall, but also the invention of the second-class ticket ...). Deeply entwined with the need to interact, and again seeded and nurtured from earliest infancy, are imitation and the delight in recognising similarities and connections. Poetry, like all other human activity, arises from the human condition. As to its specific form, one starts to produce it as graffiti-writers start, because one has seen an example and thinks 'I'd like to try that.' And you take it from there, and your idea of what the 'that' is changes with every poem you read or write."

Frederick Jones

The Wind

It could almost have been funny
so dead on the nail. The dark night
of the soul, the endless anguish,
old snake, lisping its horrible secrets,
true Lear-on-the-heath stuff

blurring without one false note
into a real storm, the worst
recorded gales in England.
Tattered shreds of sleep disperse
to focus on rows of fallen trees,

wrecked cars, houses ripped open.
an outward sign of an inward state.
Tired out and queasy the ghosts
of yesterday flit about
for phone-boxes, picking their way

among rubbish the wind got tired
of breaking. Children are thrilled
at the chaos. Worst of all
the bleak and comfortless sun casts
a naked eye on a few trees

that had stood the nightlong wrenching,
taken the shock and stood —
too weakened to be safe
they're sawn down, ruined things
unfit for their own survival.

The Institution

Another day in the hive of books'
quiet babble, the girl behind the desk
gets my parcel and I untie the string
preparing to trace through sherds of lost

collections some monk's slip of the quill,
whose Latin wasn't up to scratch
nine hundred years ago, daydreaming
amidst the whirling signs and minotaurs.

Illumination unfolds today and out
of the blue God has slopped a bucket
of sunshine through leafy windows
and unlocked and dusted birdcalls

bright as a mediæval tome of songs.
I think that in the meantime
Aphrodite passed through the office
scorching a trail of naked footprints

for now the librarian, her crotch tucked
between her legs, exudes a million volts
like ultraviolet peeling skin on skin
of a palimpsest's motley polyphony.

Congreve's Balsamic Elixir

Trapped in a warren of thoughts that hound
my steps I crawl along the pit of lime
to the Sunday Market and wander round
the ragbag of stalls. After a long time

I could still be doing the same,
sifting jumble, wondering if feeling's
returned. A will o' the wisp of calm
flits somewhere between the peeling

enamelware, the rusty biscuit
tins, pock-marked mangles and wonky globes,
jetsam whose intimations of lost hopes

and endless wear work like a vaccine.
Caught by some old bottles' milky green
I pick one up to feel, and hold it.

Ritual

A candle enters, and points of fire spread—
one flame catches even before it's touched
the last; but don't rely on it. Others
are crushed out trying to pass the light on.

Outcrop

Newcastle, after all this time,
city of girls with lovely voices,
of five bridges; theatres and bars —

thronged with crowds
of the here and now I walk about
light-headed,

absorbed in the lingering
incandescence of late growth,
the flame on the snow;

four years ·
of parties, books and music;
Turkish cigarettes,

and long games
with language. And love
which took us by surprise.

Getting on at Chingford Station

The train gags in its cat's cradle of lines.
Four down, 'the end of all aspiration',
grey minds, the end of breath, *death*, 5 letters.
I hardly notice, but for the tussle,
a schoolgirl, bland as a schoolgirl essay,

humping a cello into the carriage
She sits with a friend, and chats wide-eyed
as if nothing had ever been said before,
as if it all still needed to be said,
dictionaries pillaged. It was like

someone stepped out of the door behind me
of a Tuesday morning and switched on
the sun and then went stamping across
blank sheets of snow singing hexagons
and hockets. Before he went he cocked

an ear to their fluttery voices:
all the music I never got to play
descants out of their faces—he'd snapped off
a needle of the ice and fire of youth
and slid it under my skin. It shoots.

Hidden Pond

First there is the noisy silence
of woods, crunch and crackle of step
muffled in wads of earthmould,
birdsong like the first spots
of rain, contrapuntal, scattered.
Then the tussle with bushes,
the strangled paths and no path
actually reaching the pond.
And then you're there,
or it eludes you, and all at once
a colourless patch of sky opens
the shuttering branches.
In the still you notice,
not at first, since you're not
looking for it, that the soup
of peat and twig is boiling
worse than a witches' cauldron
with mating frogs. The thing
itself. Unenmeshed
of the day to day, the memory
hints at significance, meaning.
But at the time there was only
the moment, no truth, no symbolism,
not even a mood, like an amulet,
a pebble you pick up
and keep in your pocket.

Loose Change

My new house with its edges still
crisp as a minted sixpence — it could be
on one of the Greek islands, the backyard,

its whitewashed walls folding up the sun
and keeping it in its pocket.
With a new mathematics

it could be the centre of the Universe —
it's just how you conceive the planets,
jiggling round an orrery in loops and rings

like the holes in a pair of jeans
clumping down the steps of a bus. Three ha'p'ny
holes in the seat of someone's jeans.

You wouldn't have thought
three discs of skin could give
such a sense of a body's intimate shapes,

three coins quivering at the bottom
of a wishing well. So what if beauty
is only skin deep, if it's *her* skin.

Cairns

It starts as a game. Your son is worn out
from the steep heathscrub where the path frayed
into nothing but the odd cairn choked in ferns,
and cold with the mizzle off the fells, the damp wind.

There'd been the tarn, a grey-green lagoon
of bog-grass and moss hung between clouds and water,
the closeness at the banks, and the sodden slopes
curved round like a theatre to watch some rain

idle across the surface, far from the politics of meaning.
Twenty yards back the drizzle's almost silent
waterclock puts time under the microscope
of its atomic fizz. On the way back,

as the cold and wet sets in, your wife throws
a stone onto a heap by the wayside.
Clack and bounce. It lies in the knobs and gnarls
of pine-root pinning the needle carpet down.

When you pass a cairn you put a stone on.
It's a tradition she tells your son.
And then you're all at it, spying out
the mottled piles perched by spindling rills,

like a game in a children's picture book,
Spot the cairns in the picture. How many
can you find? One stone each clacks and clatters
and goes to keep the track for others who'll make

the journey to the tarn. And in the densest
clag of trees you seed a cairn yourselves, a few
stones each, by the stream below whose froth
you hear a deeper note as black water
tucks air beneath it. *See, now it'll grow.*

Soda Water

I'm on a bus from Didsbury Village
with a new violinbow in my case,
looking through streaks of rain at the cold white sun
when all of a sudden a tram pulls up

and I could be back in Helsinki
sitting in the Café Kappeli's huge glass bay
wondering what the function of memory is,
if it has one, if that's even the right question.

Album

Sifting the attic rubbish I come upon
an old photograph, me reading in a back yard,
and remember the smell of my wardrobe then;
after-shaves Arthurian tales could have had

in their names, *Hervis de Revel, Eau
Sauvage*, and the lists of acids we learned
at school, like oil of salts, or vitriol. Now
the sharpness is diffused and second-hand;

like that time we strolled behind some lawn
when you were five, and found an old boiler;
I saw the drum and pipes, the attractive form,
but to you it was a magic creature,

an elephant in a jungle glade. Practise,
keep your eyes open:- today I happened
to meet a palm-tree on my own, and saw it as
a feather duster turned up on end.

Mandelbrot

I have sat days at a time, charting excursions
into the empty quarter. *Mindmap:*
a grimpen, a fen, a fog, a bog, where,
short of a thousand volts or so, thought
won't rise above the stew. Tell me a lie,

something I can believe, for the syntax
of life won't bear thinking about,
everywhere weaving its labyrinth
of infinite regressions. What can you say?

'I did it all for you.' *But it wasn't for me,*
it was for your love of me, the altar
where I was victim. They go their ways
and forget. What has truth to do with life?

Nations lie, and the story sails into myth
like the Golden Hind on a sea of words,
as fluid as the air we move in. And?

Joan McGavin was born in 1949 in Edinburgh where she was educated, taking a degree in English Language and Literature from Edinburgh University at a time when Sorley Maclean was Writer in Residence. She had a year's postgraduate study at the University of California. Married, with two children, she has lived since 1975 in Southampton where she has taught creative writing to adults and English to secondary and sixth form pupils. She won 1st prize in the 1987 Southampton Open Poetry Competition judged by Elizabeth Jennings, and her poems have been published in *The Scotsman* and in various magazines.

Joan writes: "I grew up in Edinburgh. The early experience of watching my primary school burn down (Norman MacCaig was a teacher there) created a sense of the impermanence of things much at odds with an otherwise idyllic time. I later attended the school which was the model for the one in *The Prime of Miss Jean Brodie*, where love of literature and dislike of hats were fostered in almost equal proportions. Words have always been around, though: my father was a printer and used to bring my brother and I totally unsuitable 'Ex Libris' copies of books to read, and I have vivid memories of my mother and her friends composing and reciting occasional verses whilst knitting and stitching at the 'sewing bee' held in each other's flats.

"I like poems to be accessible, but not too obvious, and I'm interested in exploring the difference between the words we use and what we mean — or think we mean. I love the variety of language that everyday life throws up. For instance, if I'm teaching and a pupil who has trouble with spelling writes that the sun came 'shinning' in his window, I see it as my job as a poet to follow through the idea. Several of the pieces in this selection include words, phrases, or even lines with completely non-poetic affinities, such as gardening names, news bulletins, industrial terminology, or colloquial speech. Often it's something like this that I use as a starting point for a poem. But the poem itself has to strive for a clarity and precision that the starting phrase or idea often lacks. One of the main challenges, of course, is knowing when to stop with the idea, when it's about to topple over into literalism or pedantry or whimsy.

"Although I am, and feel, Scottish, I write mainly in standard English because I'm far enough from the way I spoke as a child to find it artificial to write poems completely in Scots. There are times, though, when there isn't an English equivalent for what I want to say, so I have to use Scots. Having this kind of enforced self-consciousness about language has been useful for writing poetry. It also helps me to adopt a different voice or different *persona* in poems. At lease two of the poems here, for instance, 'Lost Properties' and 'The Corpse Leaves Instructions ...' imply a definite persona, but all strive to shift their source in personal feeling or experience towards a more non-personal text which others could adopt."

Joan McGavin

Torn-Word*

The torn-word dozes at the root of the tongue,
bides its time, is conformable among
chat, and platitudes, and love-sounds
that do not know it's different; while round
uncurls the torn-word, syllables long.
In a sibilant sortie its carefully pronged
fangs poise themselves to slake
with gall and wormwood
the wound they first make.

* Old English: a contemptuous or scornful word; a word intended to cause distress.

In Praise of an Old Desk

If the desk that you write at develops a creak,
think what few things you can do:
you could move elsewhere;
you could rejoice (that old-fashioned sounding
word) at its animation,
that wood, hewn from something once living,
retains its vague auditory memory of that state;
you could try, chiropractically, to press hard, palms down
on its smooth or scratchy surface, to locate the spot
—but it might move elsewhere, the elusive twinge;
you could hold your breath and hope
that it might hold its;
you could shrug your shoulders, say 'So what?'
Imagine the creak was the wood
shrugging its shoulders, too, in some slow,
expansive gesture that befits
something so marked by time,
something so lined and shaped
and put upon.

On the Anniversary of the Death of George Herbert

I meant to go to Bemerton today
to walk the marches of your hard-won living
but chores and a sick child got in the way.
I cry excuse enough for my not giving
thought to what your loss of 'Court hopes' meant
and how you worked a life in its despite,
full of good use and temperate content.
Music and marriage swelled delight,
but poems measure out the journeys that you sought,
re-forge the resolutions that you hammered.
You met ill-fortune as we sense we ought,
claimed in the everyday what does not clamour —
the life quotidian, creative and not quaint,
that makes unmythed, unmartyred, the simple saint.

Lost Properties

My amber brooch is thimblerigged in leaves.
My rings are twisted into maidenhair.
My sapphires hang invisible in air.
I cannot split my diamonds from the frost.
Reset and lost; it's daylight robbery
for, clothed by Cartier, how can I
be seen in leaves, and flowers, water, sky?

The Corpse Leaves Instructions for a Working Funeral*

First, you must mend my ways.
Potholes pockmark their length,
where my enemies have been run down.
Comb the hedges and ditches;
flush my victims from under stones.
>>Tell them all to be brave,
>>tell them to dance on my grave.

Next, you must fix your sights
on targets other than human.
Contract the swollen bellies
with rabbits shot for the starving.
Restore the grain I kept trampling.
>>Tell it to grow in arrears,
>>tell it to lend you its ears.

Lastly, don't rake up the past.
Make it a quiet garden.
Re-wind the videos I took
of good men falling from balconies.
Re-build their unpieced bodies.
>>Tell them to pose and smile,
>>tell them it was all worthwhile.

* This phrase was used recently when world leaders met after the death of an
international statesman.

Explanation

That was why I was crying, as you talked on the 'phone:
I saw one image too many. I was watching it alone.
I saw a dog with only three legs, with something in its jaw.
It looked just like a bit of flesh; it caught me on the raw.

You thought that I was laughing, then; I'd changed the channel too.
You didn't see the things I saw; you weren't forced to view
just line on line of burnt-out trucks, smoke-blacked, brown with rust
and all that stuff they'd tried to take vivid in the dust.

I think it was the Carmen rollers, though, that really did the trick.
I think it was thinking of what the dog had that almost made me sick.
I think the torn huddle of bodies it was that made me switch it off —
I'm crying at this bloody traffic jam. You thought it a laugh or cough.

Gunnar Hamundarson's Stumble

We are given to understand
in small doses — suddenly, like Gunnar.
We all have a stumble like his.

Twice or thrice we know these moments —
leave a country, leave a man,
join another — no forethought, no plan.

Gunnar happened to stumble from his horse
as he quit his home at Hlidarend,
glimpsed his world in mid-air;
how precious the slope's glint:
cloth-of-gold corn, silvering hay,
lovelier than ever before today.
I am going back home; I will not go away.

The outlaw's mind was ravished,
'on pain of death' dulled over,
yet saw beyond confusion
and this is what he learned:

we may not know
when the moment of death will be;
we may choose at least its place:
our own home-field, under our own roof-tree.

The English Off-Hand Speech Competition*

That's it. I'm leaving.
So? You've been declared bankrupt.
I suppose it was the frostbite that killed him.
No. I'm not going to faint.
Yes, that was my finger in the food processor.
The Treble Chance? Well, I knew it had to be
about time I won it.
Perhaps we should get married.
Yes, I'm quite well. It's only a small cancer.
That baby doesn't look right to me.
It was a good way to go, don't you think?
With those few words.

* A Chinese student, applying for a place at a British university, pointed out that she
had won a prize in a competition with this name, in her country. I hope she'll forgive
me for borrowing the phrase as the title for this poem.

Adam's Mantle*

Adam's mantle sits on my desk,
Saint John's wort is taking over my garden,
love-lies-bleeding up the path.
Nelly Moser hangs herself over my porch,
where the baskets creak.
The ants and I vie for the dropped pears.

In the middle of it all I remember Hallowe'en's near,
and the weeding's all behind.

Hypericum's a devilish plant, devourer of gardens.
Star of the veldt also spreads mightily
but keeps flowering late, is kinder than its other name
sounds: osteospermum.
My gardening friend speaks well of blood and bone,
or is it hoof and heel? What twins!

As close as the woodbine that's everywhere this year
are good and bad twined.

It's no use banning Hallowe'en as hellish.
Domesticating the devil goes back a long way,
has a lot to recommend it. It's not giving in.
Evil's like convolvulus: everywhere, snug.
But one quick wrench and you're the one in charge:
tomorrow you'll twist, flick it away with ease.

* 'I myself have seen the ungodly in great power: and flourishing like a green bay-tree' Psalm 37, verse 36, *Book of Common Prayer*

Stuck In Highcrown Street

You shouldn't run in Highcrown Street.
Stroll or dawdle. Better, drag your feet.
Let briars do the only clinging fast
and buddleia nod as you go by,
creakingly sigh
in the long, late morning's end of playtime hush.

In the playground drained of chatter, behind gates
tarmacadam buckles in heat-rush,
buddleia leans beyond fences, manipulates
the ground, where somewhere Crump turns in his grave.
Victorianly brave,
he patented the unclimbable Improved Angle —
Iron Frame, Vertical Bar and Hurdle, Number 31.
And it works! Can trap and dangle
children stretching into branches, statues,
arrested in mid-run.

Ginkgo

for John

I pass two beautiful trees almost every day.
Casting around, in your absence, for a way to say
how I feel about us,
I think about them, I discover a fact:
their kind, fossils tell us, has remained unchanged
one hundred and eighty million years.

In the absence of tablets, stone or wax writing,
in this time of separation, of smallness of gestures,
casting around for a way,
shedding my inhibitions like leaves,
speaking for myself alone,
let's say: I feel for you what,
loving all its autumns,
the ginkgo feels for life.

Expectation—*Après Emily Dickinson*

Expectation is defined by
hope of things we can't yet see,
like the back view of an angel
or the kite's geometry.

Lovers who endure its torment—
naked swords bisect their bed—
also live by joys repeated.
Meaning stands upon its head.

Expectation is the lack of
radical impermanence
that makes the swan's reputed singing
always only ever once.

Graham Seal was born in Ruislip, Middlesex. After National Service, he emigrated to Canada, 1954. His various jobs have included: surveyor for a seismic crew in the Canadian bush; attendant in a mental hospital; technical writer. He first had a poem published in Montreal and he went on to write TV plays for the Canadian Broadcasting Corporation. His poems have appeared in *Transatlantic Review* and in the Borestone Mountain Awards anthology *Best Poems of 1976*. Several of his short stories have been published in *London Magazine*. After returning to England he wrote plays for BBC Television and one of his stories appeared in *Heinemann's Best Short Stories* for 1988. He is married, with two children and two grandchildren, and is presently living in Penzance, Cornwall.

Graham writes: "I wrote my first poem while living in Calgary between spells working for a seismic crew in the Canadian bush. Its arrival astonished me: I spent the rest of the day walking the streets in a state of euphoria at the discovery of a new self and the strange alchemy of creation: this poem was surely mine; and it was not mine.

"Since then I have branched out into other forms of writing: short stories, plays, but only poetry still has quite that unique power to surprise, with its element of grace, the something *given*. Without it the poem will not live.

"I was lucky, growing up in a time when work was still fairly plentiful and I could travel and move from job to job, browsing in libraries as I went. Poetry was incubating while my body was active and my mind in that state of abeyance most receptive to image and idea.

"Unemployment has put a check to that kind of education; and not just for the young. The dole provides for bare existence, not liberation. Hands are idle, but thought in that prison grinds remorselessly on thought. The angel enters with difficulty."

Graham Seal

Man into Billiard Ball

He was all angles, sharp as a knife,
and when, maliciously, we said:
'you'll end like us, compromising with life,'
he stuck razor blades in his smile
and chopped himself down to the bone.

He reckoned he was ivory clear through,
a sort of human dice that rolled straight sevens
by evading formulating fingers,
considering brows.

But the knocks got him, as we said they would:
it was all click clack and clippety,
there was no roll, no cushion to spin back from,
no pocket to fall into after a long white run.

So 'Make me a billiard ball' he prayed;
and we did: buffed off his chips with putty
and basted him in honey.
Such rosy ladyfingers rolled him round
he soon forgot where butter ended
and the guns began.

He was all one, circular, smooth and comfy.
The ladyfingers cooled themselves in money,
became ten white icicles moving easily
over quiescent belly; chilled him to porcelain,
blind, opaque and hard. He could see neither out nor in.

He'll run where you want him now.
For Christ's sake keep him moving,
delude him with a sense of purpose.
Intensify his love of cushions.
Whisper immortal ease into prosaic pockets.

Prepare him for another death.

They Call it Education

They have fed him Pythagorus, he knows
Boyle's Law, the Nile's source, Manitoba's
annual rainfall, which queen preceded Caroline,
who signed some declaration,
and the eating habits of the shark.

He lives on the dole and sits in the park.

He remembers fragments of Shakespeare — Hamlet he 'quite liked'
some of the root crops of Tasmania,
what stamens and pistils are, the mating habits of marsupials,
some bits of botany were 'all right.' Most of the time
he was bored and looked out of the window —
playing truant, that was a lark!

He lives on the dole and sits in the park.

His father who's worked at a job he detests for ten years,
and his mother — 'I wish I'd done something with my life,'—
made sacrifices, bought him a nice new school blazer —
'so he'd be like the others,' — got him off early
so he wouldn't miss the dates of kings, gave him
the chance we never had,'
kept him up to the mark.

He lives on the dole and sits in the park.

Three thousand good morning teachers,
eighteen thousand hours sit on your bum and get stuffed.
They call it lightening the dark.

He lives on the dole and sits in the park.

Pioneers

How did they know when to stop, the pioneers?
Water, of course. Some trees
for shelter. An acre of land
to get started. All these.
But when there was lake after lake, river upon river,
and the trees and the land went on forever—
how then?
Was it simply being too tired to go on,
a lame ox or horse,
the woman with child?

Or poetic? A sudden change in the wind's song
through trees,
or the light ceasing to fall like steel blades
and turning mellow like lyres?

Or dark coming on, and a dream
of creating welcoming lights and fires?

Or just plain bloody-mindedness,
like a coin flipped savagely inside the head
and coming down tails,
ending up with the worst scrubland for miles?

One thing is certain:
they were not interested in almanacs,
old wives' tails, the horoscope, or superstitions,
nor even most likely my fantasies—
these leathery men and their lantern-jawed wives:

The Lord would say when.

Modern Art at the Tate Gallery

Upon a broken fridge's swinging door
a string-less banjo's welded.
A black suit (wedding? mourning?)
hangs on a wall beside three blackboards.
On one is written: 'Why the poor?'
The second's higher calculus;
the third, gibberish.
I trip across a pile of builder's planks (a happening?)
and stumble on a papier-maché head
wired to a stick of dynamite.
On every wall in livid strokes
the products of distemper brushes
(or faeces-smearing by the mentally ill).
'So what?' a photo of a girl glares back at me.
I back into a face moulded in plasticine:
lurid eyeballs slide down cheeks
into a technicolour jaw.
I skirt some rubble and there's a plastic mould
shaped like a human torso, stuffed with dead batteries.
Over my head something unnameable
twists slowly on a string.

Around the wall attendants slump
guarding all this.
Their suits are crumpled cardboard.
When they yawn I see right down beyond
black fillings in their teeth
to intestines slumping into socks.
Two hands on a painted clock
are close to midnight.
Above us something unnameable swings;
tick and you're here, tock and you're not.

To His Rational Mistress

Now your house is all in order
and your judgments are quite sound,
I'll wind a cord about your neck
and spin you round and round,

Till all the colours merge, my dear,
and you can't tell white from black,
till your cries fly off at tangents
and your wits run off the track.

And I'll stop you then and set you free
in some trim and tidy town
but the street names will not focus
and you'll keep on falling down;

and the windows will be shuttered
but between the cracks, cold knives
will glitter in the moonlight
in the eyes of comfy wives.

They'll think you're mad or drunk, my dear,
or take you for a clown
and they'll send their abject husbands
to run you out of town.

And in some desert, darling,
where the cacti never flower,
they'll pin you to the burning sand
and rape you by the hour.

And when the yellow morning
slides down crouching streets,
parchment housewives will uncurl
and leave their winding sheets

and watch you crawl on burnished knees
and hear you call my name;
and they'll cut the telephone wires
and stop the only train;

and watch the desert fill your mind
with flattened empty eyes
and strop their tongues on blowing sand
and cut your heart with lies.

(On every prim and pampered lawn
starched matrons space the cockleshells,
while on the sidewalk you enact
their private hells.)

Then I'll come riding, darling,
with burnous flowing free,
and toss a rag doll on my back
and bear it home with me;

and dress it all in red and black
and hang it from a string
and teach it how to dance, my dear,
and teach it how to sing.

The Bloody Horse

I measure in thousandths not inches.
Like a wind vane I am sensitive
to the slightest wind changes
and turn my cheek accordingly.
I never make a false step, spill tea
or mention the vices of others
behind their backs. I am totally attuned,
involved to the most refined degree.
When my wife speaks I give her my whole attention.
Why then does she shout:
'Why do you never throw plates at me?
Or take me like the Duke of Marlborough
with your boots on?'

The Clown

I did not choose this role:
I too wanted the plum job, the boss's daughter,
a bathroom with mirrors.
My feet let me down: they walked before me at dances.
My hands lived a life of their own.
I was a walking time bomb.
When I arrived at parties people found they had trains to catch.
My eyes were a disaster. I willed them to look dead ahead:
they loomed out of their sockets at breasts.
I couldn't make sense of a thing. I listened to conversations,
repeated exactly what I heard,
but at the wrong times, in the wrong places; e.g.
the weather, when the talk was of God,
a shaggy dog story at a funeral.
They all seemed to weigh the same.
I worked in a bank. In three months I had given away
two hundred and fifty pounds, ten p, and the manager's house.
I worked my way up through a department store
(desperate to get to the top).
There were riots in kitchenware,
orgies in soft furnishings, and fifty-three girls left
claiming I was the father of their child.
I went to pieces in the paint factory.
I worked in baggy overalls, sporting a carnation,
and left after I had painted rainbows all over the walls.
When I got married the minister snickered,
the best man produced a white rabbit instead of the ring
and the organist played *Rock Around The Clock*.
I walked to the office like others
and was mistaken for Chaplin.
When the town hall caught fire the police called on me.
I dared not show them my fingers: they had turned into roman candles.
I inspired hatred and fear. You kept your children away from me.

Now you pay criminal prices to bring them to see me
(in their starched suits and dresses).
I watch their faces open like flowers.
When you clap steel doors clang.

91

I Have Been Innocent

I have been innocent
and smelled bread baking when cities burned.
I have walked in Adam's cool unsheared grass at morning
while napalm made deserts.
I have ducked under falling spring blossoms
when steel rained.
I have assured my children of a happy ending
as the witch and the ogre were deified.
I have pressed my nose against sweetshop windows
when the hungry tugged at my coat,
and watched toy generals play cricket on marzipan meadows
as youth was crucified.
I have handed blank cheques to fat men
because they looked like Mr Pickwick.
I have believed those who said they were building Jerusalem —
and silver loaves and fishes multiplied on the stockmarket floor.
I have dreamed in churches
as the vicar told me to love my enemy,
watching the rainbow light stream through
stained glass windows
as he blessed the troops.
I have believed in justice, in spite
of seeing corn scythed, the tares left standing.
I have seen snow falling through a tumbler of whisky,
the world white.

Take, for example, Columbus ...

You can be crossing a street
or a 't' or simply zipping your fly when
all of a sudden it doesn't matter —
where you're going, job goes phut,
wife, kids walk out on you, your whole
carefully constructed world blows up.
You can lose it all in the roll of an eyeball
or a plane of thought
as it tilts out of shadow into sunlight,
and you got springs in your heels mister
and angels' wings.

Take for example Columbus nearing America,
long blue line of a strange continent
swimming into an arc out of the radius of his longing.
Crew leaping like monkeys in the rigging,
crying, *land land land*, for them the end, new beginning,
whose heavens were all of this world.

But Columbus in his cabin maybe remembered
days when faith meant more than any land —
springing up in the grey nowhere of sea and doubt —
and he cursed the crew in the joy of his madness
and sang like an angel. Landfall, what was that?

Seeing the men chattering in the rigging,
he saw vividly the new country
under the same old human dispensation.
Perhaps he ordered the sails set about;
but the crew bore him on.
He stayed in his cabin: the best was done.

'We Are a Grandmother'

—Mrs Thatcher

Five days gone by and still no word from Hughes.
Our laureate—fat on the nation's purse!—is silent. His muse,
they say, dotes upon ageing hawks and pigs,
a fading glory. It seems
that latest scribble for the base Windsors (ah, scheming Charles!)
quite undid him. Now he pens nothing
when our baby screams.

My temper's bad. Unnatural winters. Poisoned streams.
Our meat befouled. Our emerald sea a sewer.
Our sick untended—I fly from ward to ward!
Even the light is ominous. It falls on food I eat—
tainted, all tainted! (my tasters fall like flies!).
Who will protect me? Ridley (oaf!). Lawson (that bloated fool!).
Hurd (bending with every wind!). The sheep-like Howe?

Ah, Essex, it were different wert thou here!—oh, come,
unseat my swigging husband—ring my shores again
with bristling pike and cannon; yeomen—white, all white!
My continental enemies confound—all, all! Not one a friend!

Meanwhile, no Hughes.
Too late this birth perhaps? That milksop of a son … I urged him!
My head aches. My fingers drum (all, all devolves on me!).
Only my loyal *Sun*, some trusty two or three in parliament
proclaim our birth and sing the news.
My fingers drum. I glower;
musing upon the scaffold; the chopping block; the Tower.

Farmers' Ball

They enter with a flounce of perfume,
wearing their Sunday best, though not for church,
the farmers' wives, who now I see are really girls,
wearing their subtlety of sex so gladly
I turn from my beer with a kind of rapture,
amazed at arms and breasts
also wondrously transformed.
The men are brilliantined and stiffly smooth,
sleeked hair splayed over starched collars.
They speak too loud, these men
who spend too long in empty fields,
and drink whisky like lemonade.
Fragrance of scent and powder weaves the air;
I add cigar to that, and in a sensual maze
through darkening windows watch
the slow light ebb from hill and field.
The church spire etches a darker message on the sky.
Warmth flashes between us,

the first feet fly,
higher and higher, as if to say,
'*That* for the clay!'
(though lacking clay to spite, I doubt they'd skip so high).
Beneath the spire, one by one,
tombstones gather into night;
it is remembrance of them that quickens my delight,
now, in this flesh, these faces shining for a space,
this slow, brief tilt to happiness, these waves
of mingled perfume, sweat—
we dance best between the graves.